THE BITTERNESS TREE

An Interactive Storybook for Children and Parents

Written by Mike Marsoun

Illustrated by Pearl Maxner

Design: Elusive Design, QLD elusivedesign@live.com

Spanaway, WA OrbitalMarketingGroup@yahoo.com

ISBN 978-0-578-09057-3

Acknowledgements

To Pastor Henry Wright for initially teaching us the spiritual origin of our "bad attitudes," and how it can affect our lives and health.
www.beinhealth.com

To Dr. Art Mathias, for clearly communicating the spiritual truths about bitterness in his book, Biblical Foundations of Freedom. This book is an adaptation of chapter five.
www.akwellspring.com

Finally, to my dear friend and teacher Deanne Day, for believing in the project, and for providing me with the much needed encouragement to persevere to it's completion. Also, for unselfishly donating so much of her time to edit this book.
www.restoringheartsnow.org

Dedication

To my wonderful children: Kendra, Aubrey, Makena, Marina, Lillian, and Evangeline.
This book is for you.

To my beautiful wife, Tiffiny.
My inspiration and the person I trust most in this world.

THE BITTERNESS TREE

An Interactive Storybook for Children and Parents

By Mike Marsoun
Illustrated by Pearl Maxner

Introduction

Many adults today suffer from thoughts and attitudes rooted in their response to events which happened long ago, even when they were children.

We may still be afraid of the dark because once when we were five years old, the power went out and we woke up terrified and in total darkness. Perhaps we get easily angered and fail to realize that our temper is triggered by events from our school years, when our classmates picked on us, making us feel inadequate.

For every negative belief we hold there is a cause, something we learned at a point in time when that thought or attitude took root in our hearts. How much better off would we be if we had been able to recognize those negative attitudes before they took root? Then, we could make a conscious effort to reject them, and forgive the person who hurt us. Only then would our true self, the person God created us to be, take shape and thrive.

The purpose for writing this book is so children and adults will recognize some of the traps that have ensnared them, and receive tools to avoid these traps once and for all.

HOW TO USE THIS BOOK

The Bitterness Tree is a ministry manual within a story, intended to engage children and open up their hearts. Each chapter should be read and discussed between the child and a caring adult. The adult should help the child relate the characters and situations in the story to their present day conflicts. Then, there is a "Teaching" section for the adult, to offer additional insights from the story for teaching the child. Finally, there will be an opportunity for "Making it Right" as discussed in the Q & A section, and a simple prayer that the child can say, with the help of the adult.

Remember, prayer is a huge part of finding freedom, and God is particularly interested in ministering to our pain in this way. Sometimes we can cover-up these memories that brought pain. If we pray and give God permission to open up our hearts, asking Him to show us our pain, He will reveal to us what we need to hear. We must pray and then listen for His still small voice. After all, half of prayer (the half we tend to forget) is listening!

You will see this is not a typical children's book that you can read from cover to cover in one sitting. Adequate time should be taken on each chapter to fully understand what God is saying. I suggest that you do not move on to the next chapter until you feel the child has heard from God. Or, you can read through the entire story, then go back and re-read it doing the exercises as you go. Either way, you will find that you will get out of this book what you put into it.

Enjoy the ride

CHAPTER 1
Un-forgiveness

There once was a boy named Tommy who had just turned ten years old. Tommy had a little sister named Sally who was six years old.

On Tommy's birthday he was given a kit for a model airplane that could really fly. Some of his friends had one too. They were going to start a flying club. Tommy was very excited.

When Tommy's Dad got home from work, they would work together on building the plane. Night after night they would cut out the pieces and carefully glue them into place. It was hard work, and it took a lot of patience, but it was fun because he was spending time with his Dad. It seemed like it took forever to complete, but at last it was finished. They spray painted it red, and put on all the stickers. It was finally ready to fly.

Tommy and his Dad tested it out. It flew high, perfectly straight, and for a long time…much better than any of his friend's planes. They were amazed. It was well worth all the extra time they spent getting it just right. Tommy was so happy. He couldn't wait to show his friends on Saturday.

Tommy had the plane proudly displayed on the kitchen table for all to see. Mom didn't mind because she was so proud of the work they did together.

The next morning little Sally was up earlier than the rest of the family. She was admiring Tommy's new plane. Sally didn't get to see it fly when they tested

it, but had heard how well it flew. Little girls are very curious at that age, and Sally was no different. She quickly wound-up the propeller and let it go using the kitchen table for a runway. The plane took off with a shot and crashed into the corner of the brick fireplace. She hurried to put it back, but it was too late. The wing had completely broken off. She started crying.

Everyone heard the crash and rushed into the living room to find Sally holding the plane in one hand and the wing in the other. Mom took Sally into her arms to comfort her. Tommy ripped the plane out of her hands.

Sally slowly looked up at Tommy and said, "It was an accident Tommy. I'm sorry, will you forgive me?"

Tommy looked at her with dark angry eyes and said, "NO! I will never forgive you!"

Mom said, "Now, now, of course Tommy forgives you Sally."

But, Tommy himself never said anything about forgiving Sally.

Teaching: Un-forgiveness

This is where it all starts. Un-forgiveness is the first step in an evil progression that leads to death. The entire principality of Bitterness gains authority in us through un-forgiveness. The Bible says: Make every effort to live in peace with all men and to be holy; without holiness no one will see the Lord. See to it that no one misses the grace of God and that no bitter root grows up to cause trouble and defile many (Hebrews12:14-15). This is how the black seed gets planted in our hearts. Do not let the sun go down while you are still angry: and do not give the devil a foothold (Ephesians 4:27). When we refuse to forgive, it gives the devil a place in our heart, and in that place, he will grow a Bitterness Tree…if you let him.

Tommy has pain in his heart because of the loss of his plane. Tommy loved the plane more than Sally; this is why he didn't forgive her. He prayed, but God did not take the pain away or give Tommy a new plane. Because he had not forgiven Sally, God could not answer his prayer. If I had cherished sin in my heart, the Lord would not have listened (Psa. 66:18). For if you forgive men when they sin against you, your heavenly Father will forgive you. But if you do not forgive men their sins, your Father will not forgive your sins (Matthew 6:14-15).

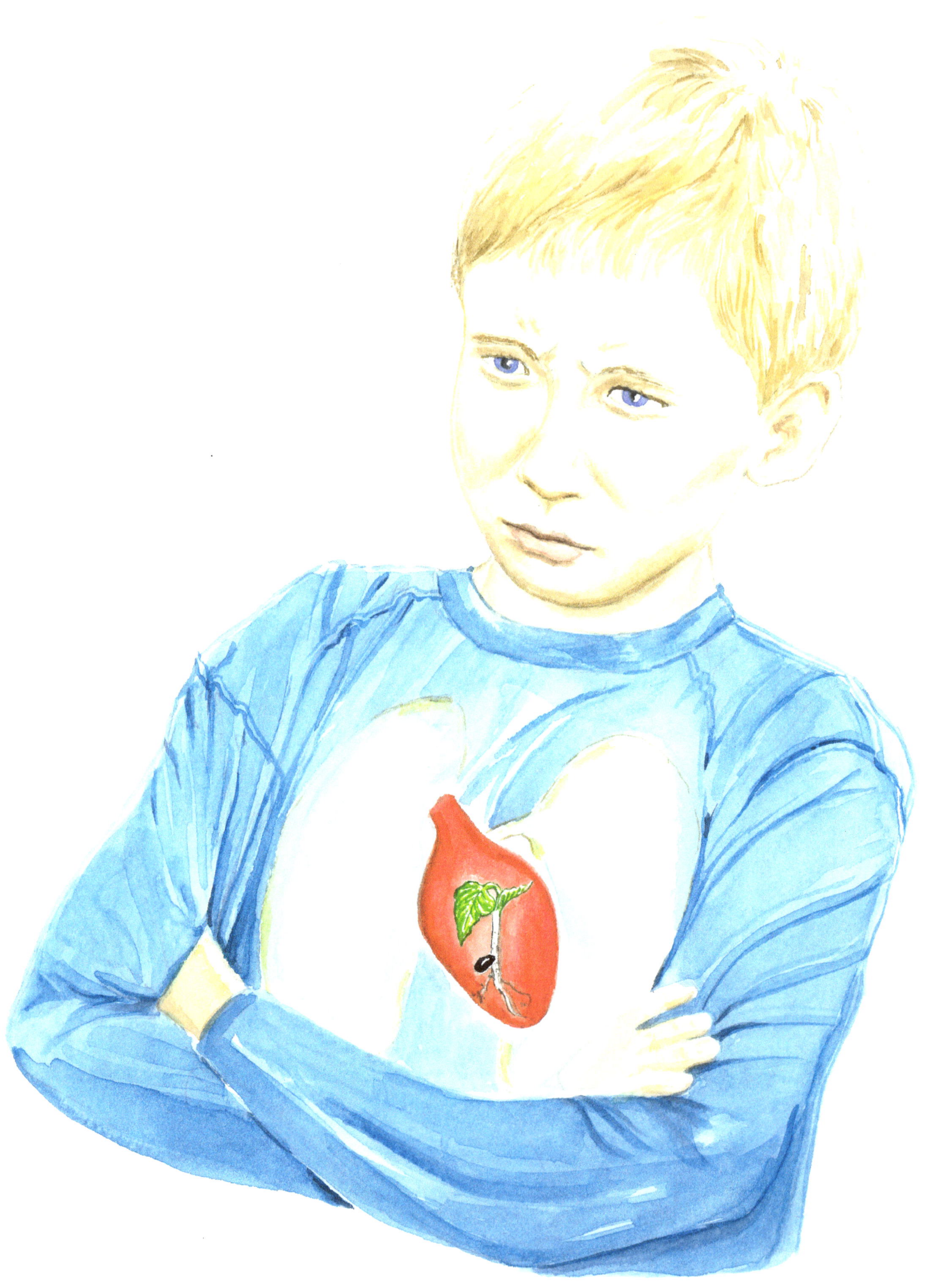

Making it Right

Question: What should Tommy do at this point to stop this trap of the devil and kill the Bitterness Tree?

Answer: Forgive Sally for ruining his plane. Ask Sally to forgive him for his bitterness towards her. Ask God to forgive his un-forgiveness. Ask God to take away the pain and sadness over the loss of his plane.

Question for you: Is there anyone who has hurt you that you need to forgive?
Pray: Father God, in Jesus' name, I choose to forgive (person) from my heart, for (what they did.) I release (person) from any responsibility towards me. (Person) doesn't owe me anything. I ask that you bless (person) with long life and your joy.

Father God, I ask that you forgive me for having un-forgiveness towards (person.) In Jesus' name all torment and crummy feelings that have come to me because of allowing bitterness to grow is to leave me now.
Holy Spirit, I invite you into my heart to heal me of this pain. Please speak your words of truth to me. (Listen. Then write down what He says.) ______________________________
____.

Walk it out: Tell the person that you have forgiven them. Ask their forgiveness for having bitterness towards them. Start thinking good thoughts towards this person so the bad thoughts don't come back.

CHAPTER 2
Resentment

Saturday morning finally arrived. It was a beautiful day. Tommy's family was all together having a nice breakfast and deciding what they would do with the day. Sally was trying harder than ever to be nice to Tommy, still feeling the pain of his un-forgiveness. Tommy looked unhappy and was quiet, still thinking about his plane…and Sally. His un-forgiveness had grown into resentment, and was about to show itself.

Just then the phone rang. "Tommy, it's for you," Mom said, handing him the phone.

The boy on the phone said, "Hey Tommy, we're going down to the park to have a picnic and fly our planes. We're going to have a race. Are you ready?"

Just then a thought is whispered into Tommy's ear, "Sounds like fun doesn't it? Too bad your stupid sister wrecked your plane. You could have easily won that race. Now you can't go, and it's all HER fault."

Tommy responded to his friend, "Sorry, I can't go. My STUPID sister broke my plane, and now I can't be in the club."
Then Tommy tells his friend exactly what happened to his plane and how he felt about it, and Sally.

When the conversation was over, Tommy slammed down the phone and stomped off to his room.

Hot

Sally was listening to Tommy talk and felt very hurt. She started to cry. Tommy's Dad didn't like this and told Tommy to stay in his room until his attitude changed.

Teaching: Resentment

The doorway of Tommy's heart has been opened by the devil who now has a legal right to be there based on the fertile ground of un-forgiveness. You see, mean thoughts and angry words are often suggested to us from the devil through the un-forgiveness that is in our heart. Right then we must make a choice to reject these thoughts. Otherwise, if we welcome the thoughts and make them our own, soon we will act them out. The Bible says, We demolish arguments and every pretension that sets itself up against the knowledge of God, and we take captive every thought to make it obedient to Christ (2 Corinthians 10:5).

We need God's discernment to know where these thoughts are coming from. If they are mean, accusing, and unloving, it's pretty easy to tell that they are from the devil, who now has a place in our heart. If the thoughts are pure, holy and loving, you know it is from God. Solomon counsels us "Above all else, guard your heart, for it is the wellspring of life" (Proverbs 4:23).

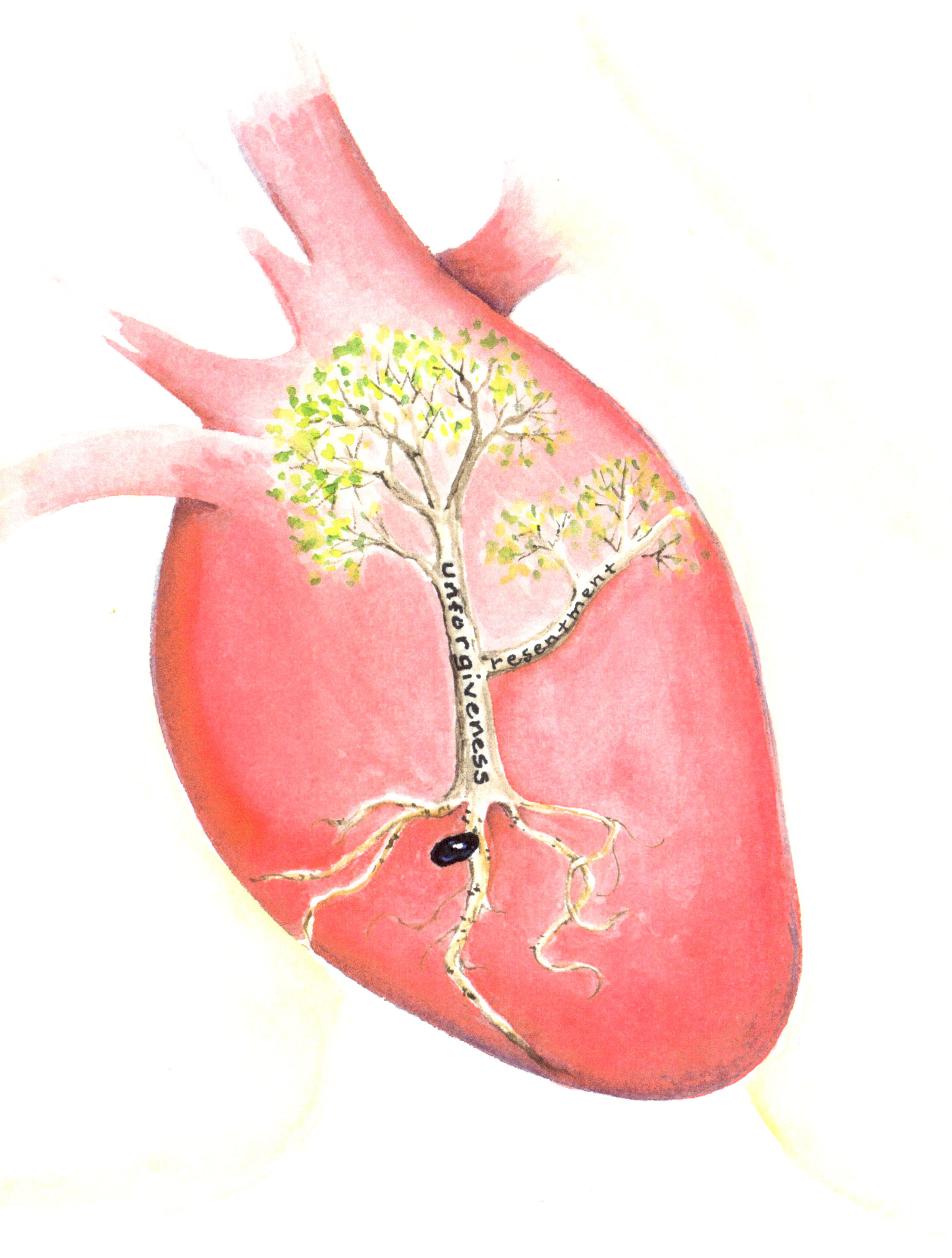
unforgiveness
resentment

Making it Right

Question: What should Tommy do to stop this trap of the devil and kill the Bitterness Tree?

Answer: First, ask Sally to forgive him for his Un-forgiveness and Resentment. Apologize to Sally for slandering her to his friend. Go to Sally and forgive her for ruining his plane. Then, ask God to forgive his Un-forgiveness and Resentment. And finally, ask God to take away the pain and sadness over the loss of the plane.

Question for you: Is there anyone you know that you are acting resentful towards? Is there someone you just don't like? What did they do to you that you need to forgive?

Pray: Father God, in Jesus' name, I choose to forgive (person) from my heart, for (what they did.) I release (person) from any responsibility towards me. I ask that you bless (person) with long life and your peace.

Father God, I ask that you forgive me for having un-forgiveness towards (person.) In Jesus' name all torment and crummy feelings that have come to me because of allowing bitterness to grow is to leave me now.

Holy Spirit, I invite you into my heart to heal me of this pain. Please speak your words of truth to me. (Listen…then write down what He says.) ______________________________

____

Walk it out: Tell the person that you have forgiven them. Ask their forgiveness for having bitterness towards them. Think about this person in light of the previous chapters of this book. What else might you have to do to make things right? Start thinking good thoughts towards this person so the bad thoughts don't come back.

CHAPTER 3
Retaliation

While Tommy is in his room he has some time to think. Can you guess what he is thinking about? Correct. Sally. Like a movie playing in his head, he is remembering with great detail the morning a few days ago when he found his Mom and Sally holding his broken plane. He is remembering how beautiful the plane looked as it was soaring on its test flight. He is remembering the phone call from his friend and thinking how much fun he would be having right now, if it wasn't for HER. He then decides to get even with Sally, and make her sorry for what she did.

Just then Tommy's Dad comes to the door and asks, "So, how are you doing Tommy? Are you done pouting over your plane?"

Tommy said "Yes," but it wasn't the truth.

Mom thought it would be a good idea if Tommy played with Sally for a little while to "patch things up." Sally is playing with her favorite doll that she takes with her everywhere. Tommy gets an idea, "Hey Sally, can I see your dolly?" Sally is delighted Tommy is finally speaking to her and says, "Sure Tommy!" and hands him the doll.

Tommy says, "Let's see if your dolly can fly as well as my plane did." He starts swinging the doll by the arm around and around, faster and faster, when all of a sudden the arm rips off, and the doll is sent flying through the air.

Sally screams "My dolly!" Tommy says, "There, now we're even," and throws the arm to the ground.

Sally's Mom comes to comfort her and makes Tommy apologize. Tommy apologizes, although not with his heart, and says, "I'm sorry Sally, will you forgive me?"

Sally's response is like Tommy's, "No! I will never forgive you!" Then Tommy's Dad arrives and leads him into his room for some discipline.

TEACHING: RETALIATION

Un-forgiveness and Resentment keep a "record of wrongs" and love us to entertain mean thoughts towards another. These thoughts are fertile soil for the Bitterness Tree to grow, adding its next branch, Retaliation. Retaliation remembers and makes vows to get even.

When we see Retaliation, we know that the Bitterness Tree is growing stronger, with the limbs of Un-forgiveness and Resentment already well-formed.

The branch of Retaliation then grows, watered with the lie "if I get even it will make me feel better." Retaliation promises comfort, but always fails to deliver. Retaliation is where Un-forgiveness and Resentment turn from thoughts into actions to the intentional harm of others, thus fulfilling scripture "…to cause trouble and defile many." (Hebrews 12:15). When these actions are carried out, someone gets hurt and their response (if they also do not forgive) can be very similar to those of the injuring party. The Bitterness Tree can now reproduce itself through Sally, who now also has the black seed of Un-forgiveness growing in her heart.

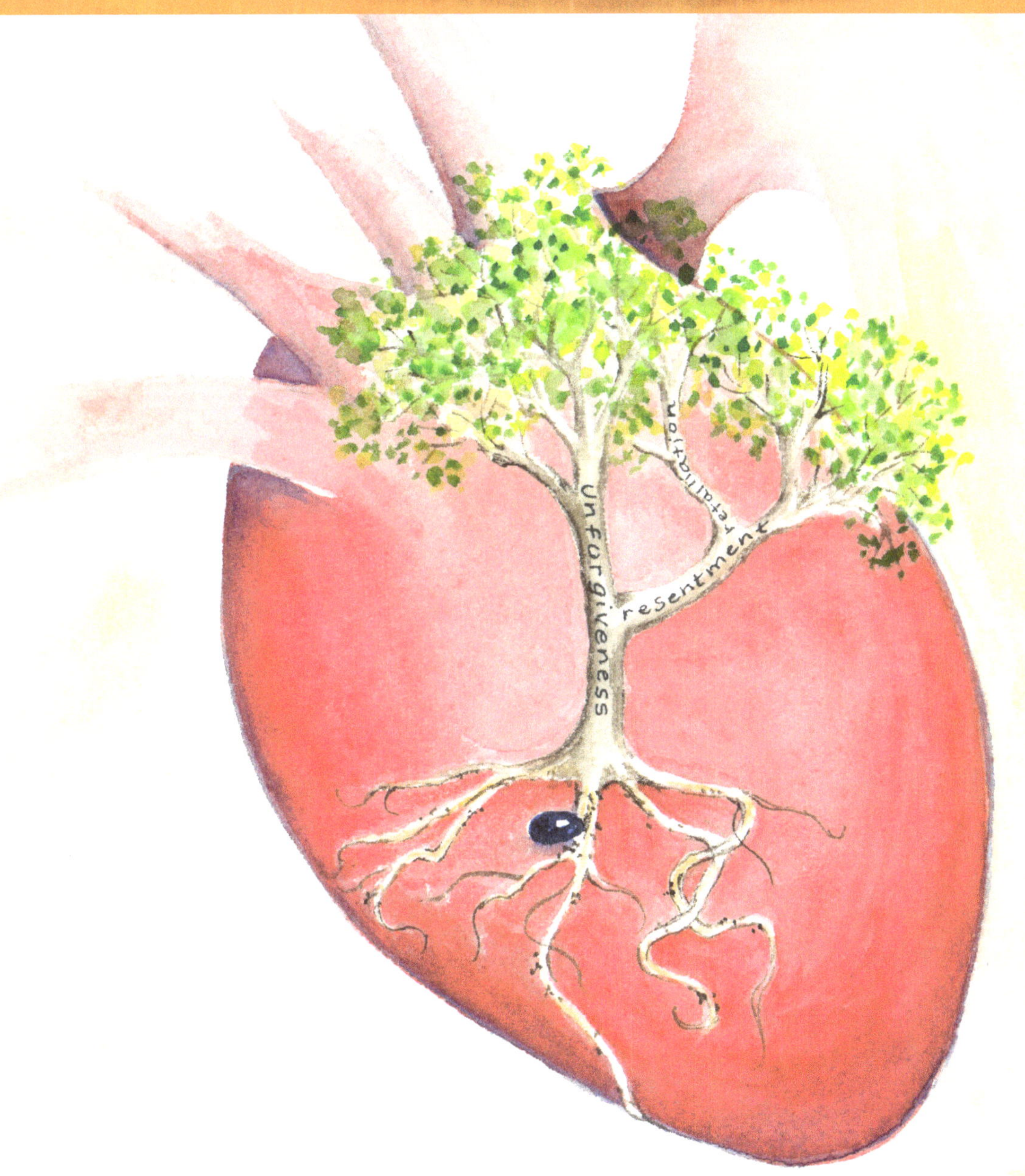

Making it Right

Question: What should Tommy do now to stop this wicked trap of the devil and kill the Bitterness Tree?

Answer: First, ask Sally to forgive him for his Un-forgiveness and Resentment, and for ruining her doll. Make it right (restitution) by fixing or buying Sally a new doll because he did it on purpose. Go to Sally and forgive her for wrecking his plane. Then, ask God to forgive his Un-forgiveness, Resentment and Retaliation. Finally, ask God to take away the pain and sadness over the loss of the plane.

Question for you: Is there anyone you know that you are retaliating against, that you feel you need to "get even" with? Why do you dislike them? What did they do to you that you need to forgive?

Pray: Father God, in Jesus' name, I choose to forgive (person) from my heart, for (what they did.) I release (person) from any responsibility towards me. (Person) doesn't owe me anything. I ask that you bless (person) with long life and your joy.

Father God, I ask that you forgive me for having un-forgiveness towards (person.) In Jesus' name all torment and crummy feelings that have come to me because of allowing bitterness to grow is to leave me now.

Holy Spirit, I invite you into my heart to heal me of this pain. Please speak your words of truth to me. (Listen…then write down what He says) ______________________________

____.

Walk it out: Tell the person that you have forgiven them. Ask their forgiveness for having bitterness towards them, and whatever you did to them in retaliation. Think about this person in light of the other chapters in this book. What else might you have to do to make things right. Start thinking good thoughts towards this person so the bad thoughts don't come back.

CHAPTER 4
Anger

It has now been a few weeks since the loss of Tommy's plane. He is not constantly thinking about it anymore, but something has changed. Tommy, who used to be a gentle and kind little boy, is now easily angered and has a quick temper with everyone. He shows no kindness at all towards Sally and is mean to her every chance he gets.

One day after school, Sally is having a tea party with two of her friends and some of her dolls. They are pretending the dolls are their daughters. The girls set up the play table with a pretty blue tablecloth and Sally's tea set, which Mom filled with raspberry tea. They were having a great time having tea and cookies, laughing and pretending. Mom was glad to see Sally smiling once again.

Tommy was sitting on the front porch feeling sorry for himself. Some of his buddies went to go play, and they didn't even invite him. You see, Tommy has not been much fun to be around lately, and it was easy for his friends to "forget" to include him. Tommy was jealous of their airplane races. He was thinking bitter thoughts against them and they could tell, even though Tommy never said anything. Tommy is now also feeling very hurt and left out, just like Sally.

Tommy could hear the girls inside the house giggling and pretending to be moms. They really did sound happy, like they were having a lot of fun. Just

then another thought comes to Tommy and says, "How come I don't get to have any fun? Why does Sally get to have fun when she does not deserve it because of what she did to me?" Tommy accepts this thought, and Anger comes in.

Then, as if someone pushed a button, Tommy's whole face changes. His eyes become dark and mean, and he clinches his teeth. Tommy suddenly feels a rush of power flow through his body. He cannot sit still anymore. He enters the house and storms towards the girls saying, "Get out of my way! I'm going to my room!" He walks in to the table, knocking everything off and making a terrible mess.

All the girls scream. Tommy looks back with a scowl and says, "Hey Sally, how come one of your dolls only has one arm?"

Sally starts to cry.

Teaching: Anger

Anger is the first branch on the Bitterness Tree from the limb of Wrath. Each branch that grows is more destructive than the others. As the tree grows, it becomes more and more powerful and evil. On this limb of Wrath, these evil attitudes manifest in ways you can easily see, where attitudes become actions and people become dangerous.

Anger feeds off of Retaliation, Resentment, and Un-forgiveness. Anger reminds us of these past events and vows. Anger is also a "false comforter," giving a feeling of power and control. Retaliation says, "We will make her pay for this," and Anger says, "I will energize you and give you everything you need." This is where people can get hurt in many ways, emotionally and physically. The Bible says: Get rid of all bitterness, rage, and anger, brawling and slander, along with every form of malice. Be kind and compassionate to one another, forgiving each other, just as in Christ God forgave you. (Ephesians 4:31-32) Also, "Do not let the sun go down while you are still angry: and do not give the devil a foothold." (Ephesians 4:27)

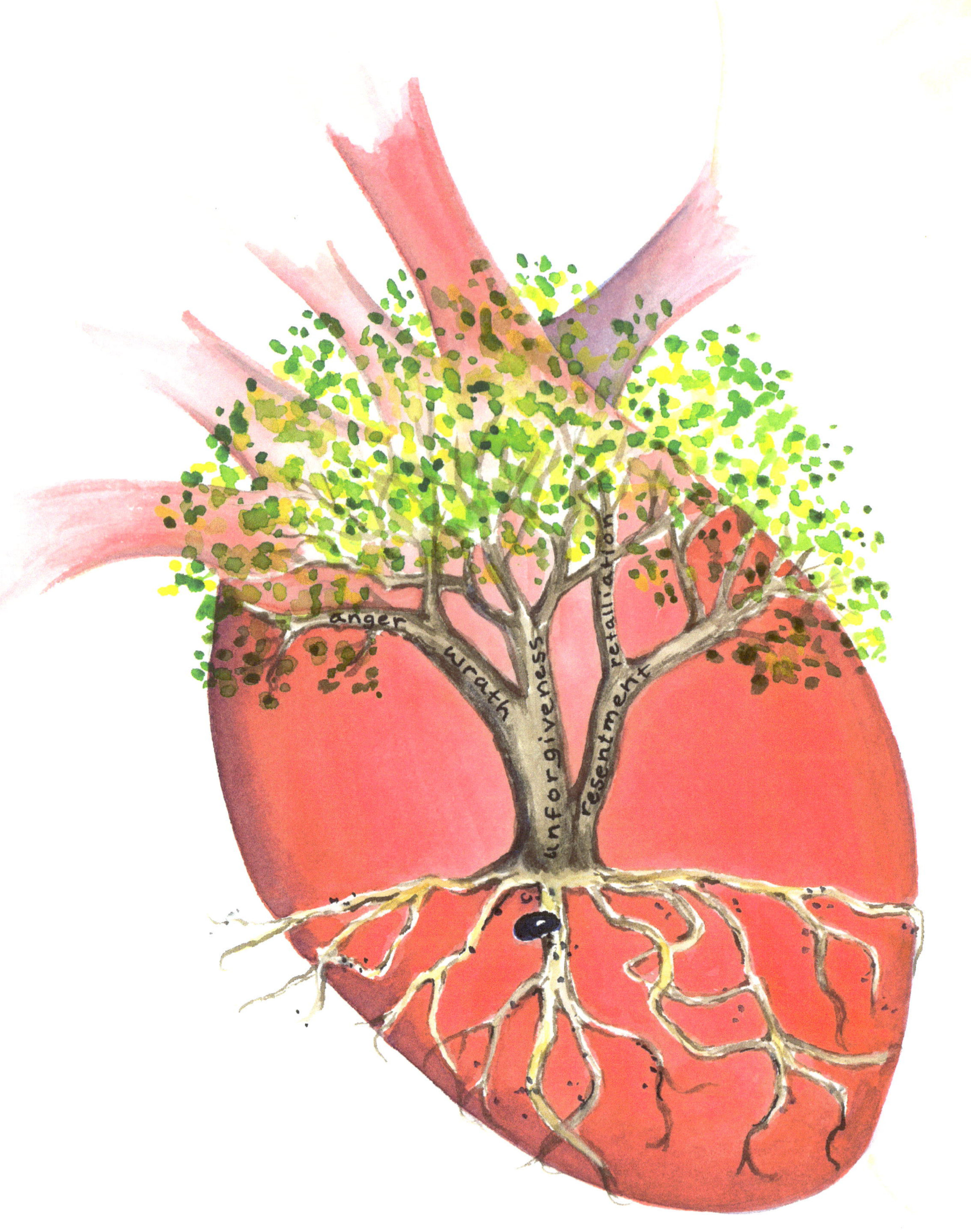
anger
wrath
unforgiveness
retalliation
resentment

Making it Right

Question: What should Tommy do now to stop this wicked trap of the devil and kill the Bitterness Tree?

Answer: First, ask Sally to forgive him for his Un-forgiveness, Resentment, and Retaliation, and for ruining her doll and tea party. Make it right (restitution) by fixing or buying Sally a new doll, and by hosting the girls another tea party. Go to Sally and forgive her for wrecking his plane.

Then, ask God to forgive his Un-forgiveness, Resentment, Retaliation, and Anger. Ask God to forgive him for his Bitterness towards his friends for not including him in their play times, and for feeling rejected and left out. Ask God to take away all the pain and sadness over the loss of the plane.

Question for you: Is there anyone you know that you are angry with? What did they do to you that you need to forgive? Do you remember when it all started?

Pray: Father God, in Jesus' name, I choose to forgive (person) from my heart, for (what they did.) I release (person) from any responsibility towards me. (Person) doesn't owe me anything. I ask that you bless (person) with long life and your joy.

Father God, I ask that you forgive me for having un-forgiveness towards (person.) In Jesus' name all torment and crummy feelings that have come to me because of allowing bitterness to grow is to leave me now.

Holy Spirit, I invite you into my heart to heal me of this pain. Please speak your words of truth to me. (Listen…then write down what He says) ________________________________

____.

Walk it out: Tell the person that you have forgiven them. Ask their forgiveness for having bitterness towards them, and whatever you did to them in anger. Think about this person in light of the other chapters in this book. What else might you have to do to make things right? Start thinking good thoughts towards this person so the bad thoughts don't come back.

CHAPTER 5
Hatred, Violence and Murder

After wrecking Sally's tea party, Tommy was once again taken aside for some discipline. This discipline was more firm than all the other times because his behavior was getting worse. His Father was getting angry, and didn't know what else to do.

Now Tommy's attitude towards Sally is worse than ever. He can't even stand to be in the same room with her, and he lets her know it. He ignores her at school and teases her whenever he gets the chance, doing exactly the opposite of what a big brother should do.

He is also rough towards her at home, pushing her around, poking and slapping her when his parents aren't looking. And he is not fooling around, he is angry.

Sally tells her parents about Tommy hitting her. Again, Tommy is taken to his room for some discipline shouting to Sally, "I hate you! I hate you! I wish you were never even born!"

Tommy's dad was trying to help the only way he knew how. Unfortunately, he had not been teaching Tommy about what was going on inside of his heart. Discipline without instruction does not train a child, but only feeds Bitterness. "Fathers, do not exasperate [provoke to wrath] your

children; instead, bring them up in the training and instruction of the Lord."
(Ephesians 6:4)

Teaching: Hatred, Violence & Murder

Tommy has allowed Bitterness to fully manifest in his actions through Hatred, Violence, and Murder. The Bitterness Tree is now fully formed and bearing fruit, causing all types of harm to Tommy and others around him.

Hatred openly and publicly expresses its feelings towards a person. It tears down, despises, stomps on, and generally seeks to destroy the other person. Hatred says, "I don't even want you breathing my air. Get out of my life!"

Violence is the physical expression of Anger, and puts Hatred in motion. Violence is represented by physical, and/or sexual abuse. In Violence tantrums erupt; fists fly, kitchen utensils fly, and people get hurt. When Tommy wrecked the tea party, his anger had already erupted into violence, and it sure was ugly.

Murder can be directed at a person's soul as well as their body. It comes from having the same attitude that would kill if a person thought he could get away with it. Have you heard the expression, "If looks could kill…?" Well the Bible says, Anyone who hates his brother is a murderer... (1 John 3:15). If someone says, "I wish you were dead" or "I wish you were never born," that person is a murderer.

As the Bitterness Tree continues to grow, its roots enter deeper inside of Tommy and can now manifest in various forms of spiritual, emotional, and physical torment. Tommy is now in a place that is dangerous to himself and to the people around him…because "hurting people, hurt people." Make a tree good and its fruit will be good, or make a tree bad and its fruit will be bad, for a tree is recognized by its fruit. (Matt. 12:33)

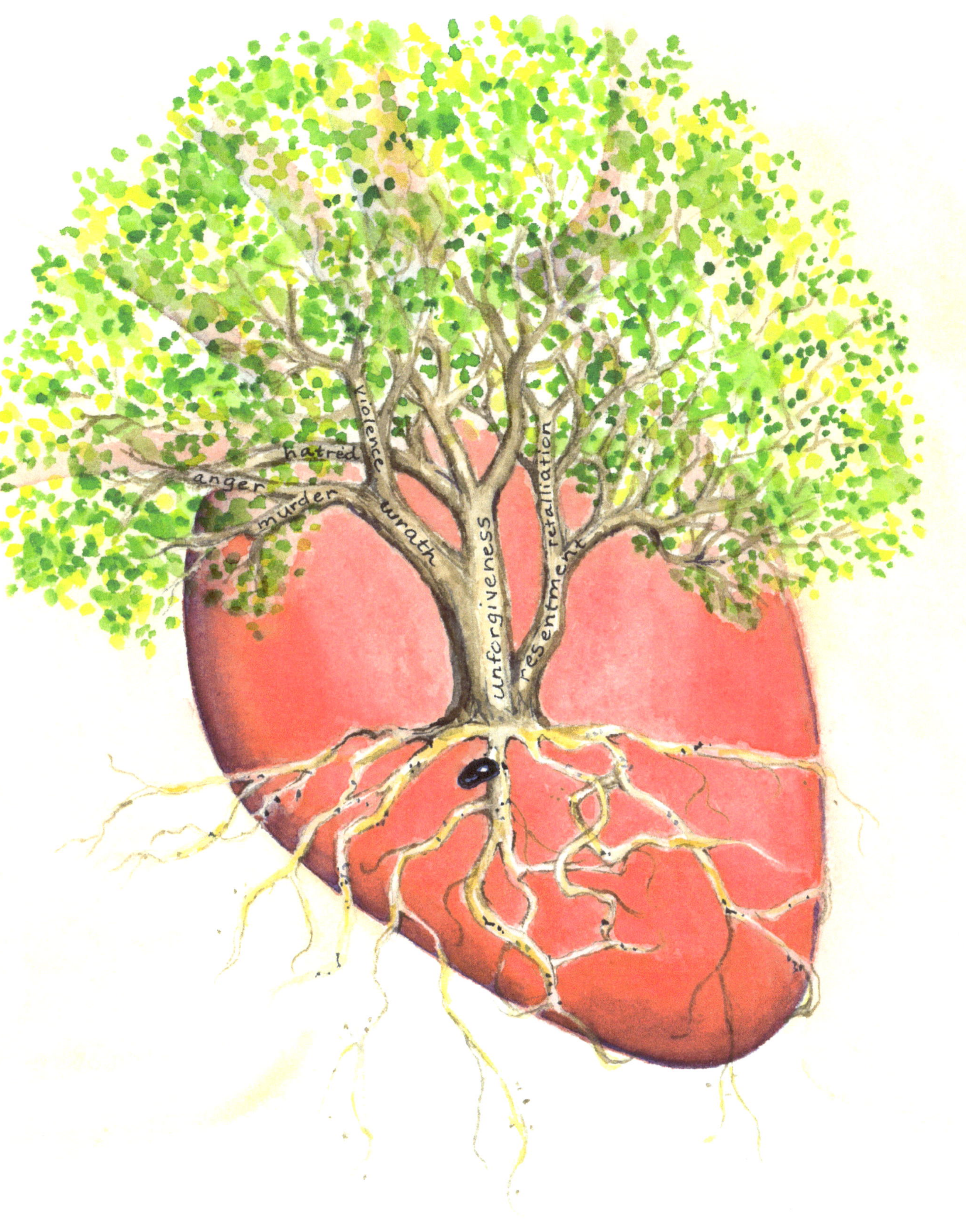
violence
hatred
anger
murder
wrath
unforgiveness
retaliation
resentment

Making it Right

Question: What should Tommy do now to stop this trap of the devil and kill the Bitterness Tree?

Answer: First, ask Sally to forgive him for all his Bitterness towards her. Pay Sally back for any of her property he has damaged. Go to Sally and forgive her for wrecking his plane. Then, ask God to forgive his Un-forgiveness, Resentment, Retaliation, Anger, Hatred, Violence, and Murder. Ask God to forgive him for all his Bitterness towards his friends for not being included in their play times, and for feeling rejected and left out. Ask God to take away all the pain and sadness over the loss of the plane.

Question for you: Is there anyone you know that you would never want to see again? Or someone you have been violent towards? What did they do to you that you need to forgive? Do you remember when all this started?

Pray: Father God, in Jesus' name, I choose to forgive (person) from my heart, for (what they did.) I release (person) from any responsibility towards me. (Person) doesn't owe me anything. I ask that you bless (person) with long life and your joy.

Father God, I ask that you forgive me for having un-forgiveness towards (person.) In Jesus' name all torment and crummy feelings that have come to me because of allowing bitterness to grow is to leave me now.

Holy Spirit, I invite you into my heart to heal me of this pain. Please speak your words of truth to me. (Listen. Then write down what He says) ________________________________

____.

Walk it out: Tell the person that you have forgiven them. Ask their forgiveness for having bitterness towards them and whatever you did to hurt them. Think about this person in light of the other chapters in this book. What else should you do to make things right? Start thinking good thoughts towards this person so the bad thoughts don't come back.

CHAPTER 6
Forgiveness

Now it is several years later. Neither Tommy nor Sally are doing very well. Tommy is mean, angry and does not like people very much. He has been in very poor health, and the doctors don't know why.

Sally is depressed. She has been hanging out with the wrong people, using a lot of drugs and alcohol to try to end her pain. Tommy cursed her when he said, "I wish you were never born." Sally did not know it was a lie; and now she is living that lie. She lives her life as if she were dead, not caring about herself or anyone else.

One evening Sally was driving home. She was on drugs, and drunk on alcohol. Her car swerved off the road and crashed straight into a tree. She was taken to the hospital in very bad shape. The doctors didn't know if she would live or die.

Tommy's parents called to tell him the news. They asked him to come to the hospital right away. They said, "Sally may be dying very soon." Tommy thought it was strange that he did not feel sad about the news, and made his way to the hospital.

When he arrived, he found his parents in the waiting room. He could see they had been crying. They were upset as they were considering the loss of their daughter, with so much sadness in her life.

12
12

The nurse asked Tommy if he would like to see his sister. Tommy shrugged his shoulders and casually said, "Okay."

Tommy entered the room to find Sally asleep, bruised, bandaged, with tubes coming out of her arms, and wearing an oxygen mask. Tommy was shocked to see her this way. He thought of her as a little girl and remembered how mean he was to her, for reasons that were really not her fault.

Tommy suddenly felt sorry for her and said a little prayer, "God, I'm sorry for being so mean to Sally, please make her get well." Just then, something in Tommy clicked, and his heart suddenly changed. He realized that he really DID love her.

For the first time in many years he cried…cried like a little boy who had just discovered a great loss.

Tommy thought that Sally would die, and he might never have a chance to tell her, "I'm sorry." Tommy always knew deep inside that he was wrong, but he could never admit it. He thought he had plenty of time to make it right, after Sally suffered a *little* longer.

But now it looked like his time had run out. Tommy cried. He prayed again, "God forgive me for being so mean and cruel to Sally all these years."

Two days had passed. Sally was still in the hospital fighting for her life. This gave Tommy plenty of time to pray and reflect on how he had treated Sally. God was speaking to his heart. Then Tommy remembered…THE PLANE! That's when this all started, with that stupid plane!

Tommy felt an immediate need to make it right, but how could he do that? He could not ask her forgiveness when Sally could not hear a word he said. He thought, "I have to do something about this." Tommy has an idea, and gets straight to work.

Another week passes. Sally is still in the hospital, refusing to wake up. It seemed that being asleep like this suited how she felt. Tommy made frequent visits bringing her flowers, balloons, and other gifts. He did have some things to say and he very much hoped she could hear his words. Sometimes he thought she could hear him, other times he just didn't know.

That week Tommy worked around the clock to make her another gift, but this was more than a gift, more like an offering. It was a plane, exactly the same as the plane from so many years ago. When Tommy delivered it to her room, he just left it on her lap, and simply said, "Sally, will you please forgive me?"

Early the next morning Tommy received a call. It was his Dad saying, "Please come to the hospital right away." Another wave of grief came over Tommy, "This is it, now I will never get to tell her what I have to say." When Tommy arrived at the hospital he didn't see his parents whom he was expecting would give him some bad news. The nurse said "your parents are in Sally's room." Tommy took a deep breath and went in. He found Sally sitting up in the bed and holding the plane. She strained to make a smile. With tears welling up in her eyes she whispered, "Thank you Tommy. I forgive you."

Teaching: Forgiveness

When Tommy saw his sister all broken and bandaged he realized that this was NOT his hope for her, and that he had believed a lie. He found that he really did love her, and "love covers over a multitude of sins." (1Peter 4:8). All of Sally's apparent offences against Tommy suddenly didn't matter anymore.

When Tommy was confronted with this truth, he knew he had to take action. He was now desperate for her forgiveness. You see, we have a responsibility before God to forgive. When we fail to do so, we hurt others. We then become the one in need of forgiveness. Tommy was broken. Through his devotion to his sister, God could see his change of heart. Then God answered his prayers, and spoke to Tommy's heart about the past.

Tommy then built a plane for Sally. He tried to make it exactly like his plane from so many years ago, giving her a symbolic offering was all he thought he could do. Even though it was not necessary, it showed Sally that he put a lot of thought into it, and he really did care. Sally could now see how much she was loved.

Sometimes, doing a certain deed, or offering a small token like this can help. It can attach a symbol to the act of forgiveness that has already taken place. This can cause a touch-point for healing that can be very powerful, but can never replace the words "will you forgive me?"

FINALLY

Both Sally and Tommy are happy and free because the Bitterness Tree, that had grown so large, was finally dead. You will be happy to hear that Tommy and Sally are now best friends and getting along wonderfully.

Sally is no longer hanging out with her old friends, drinking alcohol and doing drugs.

Tommy is much nicer, his health has improved, and he has learned to appreciate his friends and family like never before.

At last, they are both peaceful and happy. They can now live their lives to the fullest, and fulfill Gods calling for them to love one another.

www.ingramcontent.com/pod-product-compliance
Lightning Source LLC
LaVergne TN
LVHW070223110826
845147LV00003B/630
* 9 7 8 0 5 7 8 0 9 0 5 7 3 *